Your Luminous Self

Penny Novack

Your Luminous Self

Penny Novack

Hubbardston, Massachusetts

Asphodel Press
12 Simond Hill Road
Hubbardston, MA 01452

Your Luminous Self
© 2008 Penny Novack
ISBN 978-0-578-01906-2

Back cover design © 2008 Sundeip Arora

All rights reserved.
No part of this book may be reproduced in any form
or by any means without the permission of the author.

Some of the poems in this book were previously self-published in the author's book *A Gift For Living*, 1994.

Printed in cooperation with
Lulu Enterprises, Inc.
860 Aviation Parkway, Suite 300
Morrisville, NC 27560

This book is dedicated to all of you out there. I have no one inspiration and can name no powerful teacher above another. I have learned from literature as well as people, members of other species and strangers I met in laundromats or at grocery checkout lines. If any source can be claimed to have been the great inspiration of this book it would be Gaia Herself, or perhaps Goddess in all Her forms. The hills and valleys and plains which have given me overwhelming moments of joy, the small plants growing out of crevices of rock, the skies or the depths of a camp fire all teach me to love this world and my fellows. You are all the holy expressions of some One to Whom I owe all my consciousness of the Gods. It is this intuition which I follow.

Contents

Foreword: All Things In A Circle ii

Part 1: The Magic

The First Step 1
We Are 2
Deep Magic 3
Identity 4
The Adventure 5
Tempting the Troglodytes 6
Bright Blessings 7
I Made It Up And It's True 8
Aeolian Pipes And The Muse 10
She Changes 11
The Fool 12
Of Essence 12
You Too Can Be 13
You Are The Spell 14
To My Sisters 15
Essentials 16
I Sing The Dark 17
With A Cup Of Coffee 18
Candle 19
Sofit 20
Into Her Arms 21
Seeking Spirit 22

Part 2: Dreams of Earth

Knowing 24
Quest 24
Touch Me 24
Return to Eden 25
Re-Blooming 25
Kiss the Moon 26
Love Song to Gaia 27

Apple Tree 28
Feathers of Light 28
Earth Soul Speaking 29
Solstice Fire 30
Carrying the Sunfire 30
Lady Day 30

Part 3: Cosmos

"Nature Is The Art Of God" 32
True 32
Shattering Surfaces 34
Ticket to Ride 35
Origins 36
Telegraphing Cosmic Hints 37
Time Tarot I 38
Time Tarot II 39
Under All Are Roots 40
Free to Choose 41
Final Unveiling 42
Almost 42
Molten Wings 44
Alle Alle Outs In Free 44
Excerpts 45
Goal 46
Reassurance 47
We Have Walked Our Ways 47
Unique 48
Need 49
I See 49
Tirade 50
My Friends And All 51
Remember 52
Integument 53

Part 4: The Gods
- Oh Round Mother 57
- She Is Trying On New Clothes 59
- Crone Beauty 60
- Me 'N' My Buddy 61
- Eris Chant 62
- Crone In A Vision 63
- Mobius Lovers 63
- Durga 64
- Commiseration 64
- Facing The Dark 65
- Hail Brede 66
- She Dances 67

Foreword: All Things In A Circle

When I was a kid in the 1970s, I read everything that the local public library had on witches, witchcraft, magic, and ancient religions ... which wasn't much. There were sensational (and very unhelpful) books, there were extremely biased and poorly detailed history books, there were a few seedy spellbooks, and there was horror fiction. A budding Pagan in those days had to look pretty hard to find much of anything, back then before the era of Starhawk and Margot Adler. The only reasonably sensible voice I could find was that of the late Sybil Leek, and even she was a bit too ceremonial for my hedge-witch-longing tastes.

Then, at the end of an otherwise sensational book for teens about the historical phenomenon of witch-hunting, I found a slim end-chapter about actual modern witches. There was the obligatory picture of the thin robe-draped spooky-looking woman lighting candles, and then, tucked away on a back page, was the sheet music to a song-spell for chasing clouds away, by a "modern witch" called Penny Novack.

This I could get my junior teeth into ... simple, easy to remember, sung rather than intoned (I loved and still love to sing, as my founding of a Pagan choir will testify), and effective! The only problem was that it was weather magic, and the weather is notoriously fickle.

I saw glimpses of Penny Novack's name, over the next few years, as more books came onto the market. When I read about her in Margot Adler's *Drawing Down The Moon*, I remembered that spell and smiled. She and her husband were voices of outdoor nature wisdom in a sea of ceremonially-inspired chanters in smoky candlelit rooms. Even when the books started coming, there was little about Pagans and witches who lived in the wild, or the pastoral lands, close to nature. I drank in what I could, scenting my destiny.

Years later, I attended my first Pagan gathering in 1988, with my then-spouse and our three-year-old. We both signed up for child-care shifts, and I took the kid and went to the first one. I felt out of place; I didn't know these bouncing people with their own obvious subculture.

I remember that it was drizzling a bit; as I settled my daughter and went in search of juice (an absolute necessity for a three-year-old), I heard a woman's voice singing that cloud-chasing spell, my first spell of all.

My head must have jerked up, because another volunteer noted me and said, "That's just Penny; she's singing away the clouds." Suddenly, the connection between the world I'd read about and the world that I had suddenly found myself in was made, with an audible "click" in my head. I really was part of this community, this movement, this earth-centered way of being in the world. Whatever happened at this event, or any future ones, I had been welcomed, even if Penny never knew the connection her spell-song made for me.

Twenty years later, Penny's poetry has come to our church's press, and I am proud and honored to be a part of bringing it to the world, just as what she shared so long ago, in those uncertain times, brought an early spark of magic to my life. May these poems share yet more of her spirit with our burgeoning community.

Raven Kaldera
First Kingdom Church of Asphodel
Hubbardston, MA
November 2008

Part 1:

The Magic

The First Step

This is the beginning
The spiral path
Into the Craft
Of wisdom.

The fruit contains the flower,
The flower the sprout,
The sprout the seed.

She awaits your coming
Through wakening
Through dying
She awaits your knowing
The All-Beginning.

We Are

Sparks from the flame
Spray from the fountain
Bits of weathered pebbles
Skipping down a mountain
Eddies of the whirlwind
Prints from a master
Sunny dustmotes dancing
Faster
Faster

Deep Magic

If you go deeper than the Art –
Deep, deep into dark unnamable space,
Thudding in arrhythmia of Chaos,
Threading labyrinths redundantly,
And if you are persistent –
As persistent as moons and stars
And atomic attractions and seeds –
You will come to Magic
Which is never-owned
Which is eternal
Which is you but unlimited
Which is ephemeral but returning.

If you go deeper than the Art
You begin to be comforted to know
Things really are out of your control.

Identity

Scar tissue
Will not keep you from dancing,
Unless you believe
Dancing has been taken away.
Unless you believe
You are identified
As a Scar
Which cannot dance.

Abandonment, poverty, foolish mistakes
Will not keep you from a heart of love,
Unless you believe
Love's heart has been destroyed.
Unless you believe your identity
Is the Unloved
And Unloving.

The Adventure

So, when you have learned
That the fall off the knife's edge
Into the unimaginable
Was, after all, no more than the edge
Of a curbside
And getting up again is possible...

When you have, at last, within your grasp
The naked energies of time
Sharing with you the dusty skin
Of your ripe years,
Invisibly assuring you
You are simply an aspect of the ultimate Dance,
Whatever your flavor...

When you know you are immense
And nothing, an illusion,
Will you savor
The next unknown wilderness,
The next adventure?

Or could it be the unforeseen mystery
Will metamorphose you into
Someone
You've
Never
Believed?

Tempting the Troglodytes

I draw forth brilliant skeins
Spun from the World's light
Splashing it around you
Stretching it till it drips into your eyes.
You are shackled away in the dark
And I want to set you free.
You are bound away in the cold
And I want you to step into summer.
You are caught in an illusion
Of the world
And I want you to come play.

Bright Blessings

May you be blessed
May your sorrows only lead you
Out of danger's way,
May your fortune's great good
Never chain you from life,
And may your adventures
Land you
Always on your feet;
That you may dwell in the land in joy,
That you may grow
In a sacred way
Forever.

I Made It Up And It's True

(inspired by Jean Giono)

But I didn't make it all up.
It came to me out of the air.
Its colors teased me with knowings.
It planted a star on my brow
So I could see, and I grasped it.

In my hands it was like silk
In my hands it was barbed with roses
In my hands it slipped away like rain
But I grasped it and I spun.

It fought me for pale slips of memory
Burning in my starrish eye.
It fought me for my open maw
Red and pulsing with delight.
It fought me for possession of running
It fought me for chill summer dawns
Gray under wisps of stolen light.

And sometimes I won.

I stole the sky
I stole the sun
I stole the moon
I stole flight
I stole wind
I stole the kisses of angels.

I stroked the quivering flanks of mountains
I bedded cascades of stones

I made love violently with great cliffs
I stole the deep mud of March
I stole the fertile clod
I stole the birthing sandbank
I stole my ancestors' bones of stone.

Within my womb I gestated forests
Within my breasts all were fed
Within my arms all were comforted.

It was not all made up.
It came to me out of oceans
Curing my belly with salt
Placing a living faceted sea in me
And scouring me raw in sand.

It was full of dancing but I grasped it,
I knitted it up under my heart.
It gave me a rough ride
And I wove its fruit out of my flesh
And became sea-wrack crying with gulls.

There was no rest from its thrashing
Serpentine, fragile as dustmotes
Desperate as a wounded bird
Powerful as winter-savage roots of grass
Ready to devour Spring.
It was ready to be woven
And I was the loom.

Aeolian Pipes And The Muse

We are not the authors of our art.
We are conduits for the future.
We are the answers of chaotic whimsy
To an inevitable progress of entropy.
We are the whimsical pen
Of graffiti artists
And the tiny stone
Before the avalanche.
We are plugs in the dam of time
Or the step which cracks the ice

It is not that we are not acting
But that winds blow differently

She Changes
(Second Meeting With A Red-Haired Woman)

Surprised, you say she appeared
A different way
Our meeting last.
Yes, I say, you can never tell.
Though you think yourself now to be
At a warm, light hearth,
Crowded and merry,
For all you know
You may have instead
Stopped off in the dew-cold woods
And be holding blind council
With a fox,
A crow,
And a grey-tufted owl.

The Fool
(First Trump)

You walk through quite a theatre
Of art and symphony and flow
This world a giant mobile
Balanced
With such cunning grace
That not a leaf should fall
But moves somewhat
The Earth

Of Essence

I believe in the Phoenix within.
I believe unshattered in the flame
Consuming feather and bone of life.
I believe
In the Egg of Nothing
From which springs
Wings
Of fire.

You Too Can Be

Luck
Is a kind of magic
You can learn.
Of course,
First it helps to have eyes.
First it helps to see luck.
All sorts of luck.
Reach out your hand.
Catch an edge of the world.
A *shove*
As if a window opened to let
A butterfly out.
Luck is enough to go around
But can you lead it
To room to fly?

You Are The Spell

Having grown up among family
And neighbors and things
And certain landscapes known so well
You drip essential mists of them
Wherever you go – you are magic.
A talisman prepared by your ancestors
And Earth – to fill a niche in the spell
Begun just Now, so to speak,
Of Creation.

When we mix our small spells,
Cut loose in caroming trajectories
From the Hot Shot Billards Master's cue,
Phantasms form and fill the interstices
Weaving beauty in fascinating trails of fire.

To My Sisters

You are so much more
And so much more beautiful
Than time and space
And games of mind
Could ever know

Live for yourself truly
And you will feel the world
Stretched out around you
As if nerves of light extended
From your pores
To each rock, each bird

You are the one true miracle
You are eternal
    Ephemeral
        Creatrix
            Destroyer
                Phoenix
You are irreplaceable

Essentials

It ain't no sin to take off your skin
And dance around in your bones.
(early 20th Century ragtime)

Bones of flame
    melding motion and matter
    holding
    nanoseconds
        Flesh

Bones of force
    patterning together time
    and Now
    all of love/loss
        Body

Bones of power
    travelling instantaneous
    frames
    creating
        You:

It ain't no sin to take off your skin
    and dance
    dance
    dance

I Sing The Dark

Like a river through deep woods
Full of Death and the power of Birth screaming
I sing the Dark.

It threads through
My sacred weaving.
It dances descant
To my song.

I sing the Dark
Mother-Father
Face
In the midst of gaiety –
Illumining
Illumining
Butterfly dances in the sun.

With A Cup Of Coffee

He said "You know, we aren't all
Of one piece.
We are many layers
And some parts of us
(For whatever reason) stopped
Developing..."

Describing how fear, illness, trauma
Leave us ice-locked.
Telling us where he's been,
How humbling it's been
Coming upon hibernating child-bits
Thawing in surprising ferocity.

I remember.
How long can it take
To release that shining, ordered chaos
Of our deepest Selves –
As we were meant to be?

Candle

It is my soul which burns
Spirit hissing and sputtering
Defying wind

It is my soul which burns
Clear, a teardrop white
At the core
Unmoving flame

It is my soul which burns
Tenaciously consuming the hours
And years and days
Of my flesh

I have not been lit
Only once a moon
And the match
Is not
The flame

Sofit

They may enclose this empty flesh in white
But at the end, I will go naked to my Creatrix.
And She, who is clothed in Chaos
For Her beauty's sake,
Will know me.
At the end I will be known among stars,
Will be young as wind
And will be free as Spring
And safe as home.

They may wrap this empty flesh
As they choose.
I will go naked as birth
Into the arms of God.

Into Her Arms

If She comes to take me to that Dreaming Source
All alight with rainbow Time,
She will fold me to Her breast
And I will go –
    although
        I want to stay and play.

When She comes to take me from hills and woods
Into a Garden enfolding Universe,
She will take me up in Her arms
And bid me rest --
    although
        I want to stay and play.

Soon She comes to take me
To Begin – again –
Aflame and lost from Time.
She will loose me into Forever
And I will go –
    although
        I would, still, stay and play.

Seeking Spirit

I will see you
Amid poetry and dreams,
Streaming through the fingers of trees,
Bursting from tough pink roots,
Twining among mosses,
Birthing within lairs,
Dying upon hollow flesh,
Forming from clay,
Shaping in waves of sound,
Pouring from throat and
Horn and
Chime
And flowering
And in pain
And enraged...

I will see you and our joining
Will be the moment
And our joining will be the end
And our Joining will be
The same One
Which never ended or began.

Part 2:

Dreams of Earth

Knowing

All life moves toward the essence
Of what it is.
Toward weakness, toward strength;
Toward decay, toward beauty.
The seed knows the shape of the flower
And the flower knows the taste of the fruit.

Quest

Teach me your moon-ways
And the wheel devouring its journey
A-crossing that deep web
Of that nonexistent night

Touch Me

Goddess, you are all around me
And I only awake enough
To know you a little –
But you move
And the hills are a glory,
You speak and the trees are dancing,
You touch me and I am real.

Return to Eden

This magic world tells itself stories.
Comfortably dancing its chatty songs,
We forget
We ever lived
Sterile
Static
Lives asleep
In the dream of inert, inanimate
Industrial Reality.

Re-Blooming

Out of our losses spring
The flowers of memory.
Within the dark earth
Of forgotten frustrations
Are seeds of pride.
You have survived
And carry within
The healing garden.

Kiss the Moon

She has broken
Free of that net
   of clouds
      and sails
Over treetops while we whirl...

Oh kiss the moon
   and whirl!
Leap the fire, we will,
    again
And drink May wine
   and love
But up! Up! And whirl about!
Kiss the Moon!
For She's full at May...

Love Song to Gaia

Oh Mother, you are always there
    (in your beauty, in your glory)
Shining through the universe
In bright gold days,
Greening up the tips of trees
In bare cold spring –

Oh Mother, you are always there
    (in your beauty, in your glory)
Talking through the great rocks
Towering and old,
Scenting up the dry earth
With the freshest rains —

Oh Mother, you are always there
    (in your beauty, in your glory)
Flying with the high geese,
Flaming on the hills,
Singing lullabies of sweet cold
Covered all with snow.

Apple Tree

Apple tree, Apple tree,
Home and health and hearth to me.
Apple tree, apple tree,
Seasons four and maidens three
Sing to my heart from an apple tree.

Feathers of Light

Oh I will run wild in the wood
And laugh in the velvet air
While Mother-of-Magic, the Moon
Tangles Her wings in my hair.

Earth Soul Speaking

I am speaking to you
Listen.
    You are walking in my breath
    Kicking up my dust
    Pounding in my pulse.
    Listen
    I am speaking.

Here, here in your breast!
    I am your voice
    I am your bones
    I am your gut
    Listen
    I am speaking to you.

You are dancing to me
Dancing your days;
Asleep.
Dancing dreams
You do not want
Dancing
Your voice, your breath, your feet
You are sending me
Your agony.

Listen.
I am speaking. Listen.
I reply.

Solstice Fire

Sunlit candles
Burn fast
Making
Wax waterfalls

Carrying the Sunfire

Crossing the edge of light
Between a year done
And one yet to come

We carry fire
Stolen from the sun

Lady Day

Sweet with lights they bring
Candles
Out of darkness
    Maidens
Tiny and dignified
With flowers in their hair

Part 3:

Cosmos

"Nature Is The Art Of God"
-Dante

All this is sacred.
All, all acts
Are God dancing,
Each day's dance,
God acting.
We are holy.
We are perfectly sacred
Like a leaf
Like a web
Like volcanoes.

True

True mysteries
Are so immense
That unless you feel them
Deep in your bones
They seem simple.

Brillantly Maya

Everything fails at last.
Frail as the shattered grass of drought,
Each ephemeral and vital thing
Fails at last.

Build in temporary permanence,
For winds will blow
And the rhythms of the tides
Will shake the firmest tower.

Build as writers carve thoughts
Upon a page which turns to dust.

Know your temporary mark
Of love or pride painted luridly across
The sunset sky
Will die.
And that is only right.

For every solid thing
Shall fail at last
And every great magnificence
Will come to birth
And fall
In only an instant
As stars fall
As galaxies cool
As the Dream
Ceases
At last.

Shattering Surfaces

You have seen our Shining Selves
'Neath the prisms and the patterns
Of our transitory lives,
Where the starlight of tomorrow
Rides the light waves to our past.

And, if you are not gentle,
Yet, Great Mother, you are kind
In the many ways you shatter
From a grey and faceless shape
The multi-diamant moon-stones
Which veil the Garden
In our souls.

Ticket to Ride

I keep telling you
You are the magic station
For the transfer of Time
You are the nexus
Of mythic incredibility.
Breathe it in.
Look beyond.
You are the beginning.
Each point is your choice.

I keep trying to set you
Onto the Marvel Express.

Origins

The magic world
The world of gods and unicorns
Is here, right here,
Composed of this same world,
These substances,
Energies
And shapes
We take so calmly.
Here is the Abyss.
Here is Chaos.
Here is the Song as it was first sung.

This is the universe –
Time cuddling Space
Frozen in ecstasy
Exuberance
Exhilaration
This is the universe:
The Eternal Is!

Telegraphing Cosmic Hints

Echoing
    echoing
        echoing
            echoing
                Again –

Now watch
An Orb Weaver dance
To the moth

Watch
Moths whose camouflage
Mimics communally
    a flower.

She is telling us
It is
Fun
He is telling us
It is
One

It is telling us
    "Hi, Folks!"

And laughing
    At the expression
        On our collective
            Face

Time Tarot I

It's important.
Don't tell unless
You'll be understood.
This could save a life.
It's a secret ...

Each Moment Is Complete.

Be careful how you let it out, now.
The magic trick of it is
You can pick and choose
How you build memories.

With this power you can be
Sun-filled,
Dark-shining,
Successful
Retroactively.
Don't tell
Until
You've shuffled
Your
Own Deck...

Time Tarot II

We create ourselves.
Don't be afraid to return to success.
Treasure each pleasing.
Be stern.
Refuse to avoid happiness.
Force yourself to love again.
You can survive pain.
You can survive betrayal.
You can survive most mistakes.
You cannot survive on a diet of self pity.
You cannot survive selective memories
Which tell you to give up.
To die.

Under All Are Roots

Rules of style,
Fads of mind
Ephemera of place and time
Are not
    Who
        You
            Are

Not rooted in genetics.
I am not
My ancestors
Fighting each other
To puppet-twitch
This life.
I
Have roots
In Chaos.
I
Am known
To Gods
And am
A maple
Or
    perhaps
        a mouse.

Free to Choose

You are perfectly free to choose.
You may live between the raindrops
Or slosh in torrents.
You may throw yourself into danger
Or arrive unrumpled
Going to the same place.

You are perfectly free
To choose
A world animate and numinous
Or opaque and tenantless.
You are free to choose
Logic and intuition
But don't expect magic
When you choose
An unliving world.

Final Unveiling

You can throw away fear.
It no longer matters
Whether you live or die
But how.
You need to be stubborn.
It no longer matters
What other people think.
You can give up control.
If you can steer yourself
Day in, day out
It is enough.

Almost

I am almost perfect.
On my way to forever
I am shedding time
In undulant waves
And only understand
Change.

Saundra's Gift

Never believe you leave Love behind.
Love goes before and follows after.
When lost you seem, keep in mind
Love goes before and follows after.

Paths we may take which twist and wind,
Some with tears, some with laughter,
Bring us back until we find
Love goes before and follows after

And at the end when flesh is blind
And Spirit reaches out in rapture,
Never fear, my friend, you'll find
Love goes before.
Love follows after.

Molten Wings

Speeding on the wind of light,
I saw them pass
And reached,
Dreaming I am
A Phoenix

Going away are the angels
Whose fiery feathers
Slipped softly through my hands

Alle Alle Outs In Free

When will You say to me,
"Come out, come out!
Wherever you are!"
And I will rise, shining,
From my games of form
To stand like a firestorm
Consuming
Everything.

Excerpts

...sometimes I think I'm tripping
    over life
I have Diogenes lamp and I find nothing but
Honest Men.

Honey in the hive
Hexagonal three-dimensional life
Like a pull-toy
Pulled into
    the Fourth dimension
        by
            ???
It's absolutely all as real
    as our fun-house minds can
        comprehend
This Creation is not illusion
We are
Dreaming dreams woven in ways
God couldn't have imagined
We are the graven images
We are the idols
We are God's way of thinking
the unthinkable

Goal

I knew a saint, once.
When I said, "Her soul is like wind."
I was told, "She is mad."
Mad.
Whenever I falter
In this world turned upside down
By the magic
Of words
Of things
I remember a saint
And think when I grow up
I want to build a stone home
Piece by piece on a mountain
Piece by careful piece
Emptied of words
Emptied of things.
I want, also, to be a saint
In a sacred world alive.
I want to grow a soul like wind.

Reassurance

You are intricate.
You have been shaped in little pieces
From messages sent geologically.
You are punched for passage
And will never let in
Less light.

We Have Walked Our Ways

You have walked your ways
And I mine.
Each mote of Creation
Each wave crashing
Each strand of the Web
Each
Each
Perfect.
Only one note
Reverberating.

Unique

All are holy.
There is no soul not sacred
In the Dance of Creation.
In New Hampshire woods
A sacred erratic stone
Perches above hardwoods.
Placed in the tidal dance of time,
Sacred birch and pine
Dance their quicker dance,
Lodge limbs and roots in complicity
Setting the next stage in cosmic play.
You, in your flesh and bone,
Quick with breath
Oceanic with blood
Are holy.
You are the gods hiding
Among patterns of wonder
And are the only one,
Not a copy.

Need

I have never needed my religion
To be
Just good clean fun

I See

I see, each of us,
Poised,
Falling.

I see, each of us,
Poised,
Dancing.

Tirade

You frighten me.
Yes! You!
You do not value yourself
In the world well enough.
You do not value yourself
In the future enough.

You frighten me.
You do not believe in yourself.
You do not remember
How creative,
How beautiful,
How loved,
How important
You are.

My Friends And All

Each is
Not without flaw –
Each fragment fitting
Intricate puzzles of existence
With
Flaws –
Hiccups in the process
A perfection of chaos
Building an Order
Of change
Change
Change

We are all dancing in Free Fall,
Gloriously flawed

Remember

In every hour we must choose
How we will remember ourselves.
Will it be as a heart of shadows?
Or brightness wide as Earth?

Behind the veils of tears,
Hidden by fog of despair,
Darkened by abandonment,
Wandering among echoes of anger and pain,
Remember –
Behind
Is radiance.

Remember
You are not only what happens.
Remember
You are not only your acts.
Remember
You are not only today.
Remember
You are based in magic.
Remember
You are spun from flame.
Remember
Return
To your Self
Shining in scintillating laughter
Holy
And free.

Integument

There is no fabled land of riches but resides within the skin:
Skin of flesh from which our wounds pour rivers of sorrow
In seas of air, mating air and closing wounds.

There is no fabled land of riches but resides within the skin:
Skin of sea in love with air, held to Earth's sweet basins,
Awash and pouring Her Spirit into clouds, reaching out to Sun
Racing the moon and falling, falling into far places.

There is no fabled land of riches but resides within the skin:
Alight with solar chemistry, breathed by all of Gaia, air itself
Stays barely within it's skin – but stays and moves and lives
Changing all within itself and leaking bits of stuff
While gathering visitors from far space, moving, restless
And filled with wonder.

There is no fabled land of riches but resides within the skin:
Skin of such fragile frame written on the skin of time itself,
Each ephemeral glory lasting as an exclamation point.

There is a story that, initially,
A wounding of the perfect silent Universe
Became a Word before words were born.
So implied within that ordering explosion were all worlds and
A clotting of the leaking forth of Self which simply was.

We are all dust and air and water and time and space and yet
Only ephemera writ with one sweet Word
Upon the skin of the Creatrix.

Part 4:

The Gods

Oh Round Mother

Close your eyes
Listen
Swirling between thin solar energies
And green-mossed stones
Winds perform wild dances of love
Circular, lush, filled with Her arms,
Wild as Her primal energy.

Close your eyes
Smell
Earth wakening in Spring – Autumn leaves,
Stone-scented springs gushing
Love-messages flowing from flesh, from flower,
Her plump fragrant messages
Lusciously wild and wet.

Close your eyes
Touch
Contours of tree-flesh, leaf and root
Stones stream-laved, fruit hanging ripe.
She is round and soft, curved and hard.
Oh Round Mother! Oh lush Beauty
Perfect and full of Life!

Open your eyes
See
In full richness She plays before you..
She is dense and soft and glorious
Lovingly sweet, rough as waves,
Intimate as grass stains,
Warm as bonfires, cool as snow.

Lift up your arms, Round Woman, dance!
Toss your head, Oh Mare of Wildness, dance!
Be filled with glory, Lush Undine, dance!

Oh Round Mother, be me.
I who am only a raindrop of Your rainbow curve,
I who am only once in Your Always,
Let me rejoice in my flesh
Let me be apples and honeybees in your heart.
Let me be proud,
Your sensuous beloved
Daughter!

She Is Trying On New Clothes

That scintillant dance of Patterning laughs.
Trying on New Clothes, Goddess Tosses a veil;
It becomes a skirt, a toy, a bodice.

Her long rivers of hair move into the sky
She laughs and Her breath is birds, carrying memories.

All that is Old has become New.

Archetypes move over and welcome new visions
Making love to poets and artists who swim
In creative seas.

All that is New metamorphoses from Old.
There is no wrong art
There is only transformational truth
Or meaninglessness
Dream
Dance
Paint the flowing substance of the Heart
Brightly
Exuberantly
On the wing.

Crone Beauty

When I visualize my favorite Goddess, Eris,
Playing hide and seek within
Tidal-atomic winds
Of space and time,
She has the vigor and arrogance of youth.
Nonetheless, She who moves, thus
Dancing Manifestation,
Is more Crone than Kore.

There is a beauty
Only attained
With well-earned age,
A wisdom which is freer than innocence,
More open than naivete
And an in-depth unconquerable beauty
Which stems
From Spirit shining through
Unafraid.

Eris, laughing anarchos!

She is the Core
Not the Kore.
Unmoving, forever in motion
She is the Self-Woven
Web of all realities
And She is proof to all who seek Her
That we are free.

Me 'n' My Buddy

She laughs at me, that Crone.
I get no respect.
I ask Her questions
and She laughs.
"You already know the answer to that,"
She says
And laughs.
She's right.
She lets me know
She needs me
Whenever She needs
A good laugh.

Eris Chant

I am change
At the core of Chaos
I am wind
Birthed twixt Earth and Sun.
I am the unborn
Forming in God's Eye.
I am the fulcrum
Whence Luck moves in balance.
I am the dance
Asleep in music's weave.
I am the dark
Created by light.
I am the story
Yet to escape into telling.
I am pain
I am joy
I am the vital force
Moving like a flame
Calling in the wilderness
Promising
Your deepest heart---
If you only ask
The right question.

Crone In A Vision

She said, "Look at me
I had quite a body
Once."
I believe
She is powerfully
In possession
Still.

Mobius Lovers

Profligate Creatime –
Profligate sowing worlds
Within worlds
Whirling past Herself
Too fast to kiss
Within His spiral counterspin
One embrace
Never begun, never ending

Durga

I have forgotten I am you.
Under my blade your thousands shatter
Within my flames your screaming breaks
Beneath my feet your unknown souls
    lie dazed
And I cannot rid myself of the cosmic itch
Of your deaths

Commiseration

I'm sorry you believed
GOD
Had to be nice

Facing The Dark

I am the Sow.
Terrible in my love, I eat my brood.
Protective of my sickling young,
I return them
to my Self.
I am the Sow.

I am the Farmer.
Grim before blight
I plow the summerfield,
plow under the crop.
I am the Farmer.

Durga am I.
Leaping from the chains of Love,
I slay
Creation up to The Self of Love.
I am Durga.

Death I am.
Life I am.
Dancing
Walking
Falling
Flying
You will face me.

Hail Brede

Brede of fire
Brede of flame
Melting thought
Moulding song

Brede of Bards
Brede of Smiths
Hammering iron
Moulding gold

Winter-change Brede
Weird of the Boundaries
Cradle of Inspiration
Brede who sets to forge
The Fates, the Muses
And the creation
Of the soul

She Dances

Her hands inextricably bound to ascent, descent, tipping
Absolutes into the unknown and juggling –
Juggling illusions more real than real,
More fatal than birth,
More beautiful than
Having it all under control.

She dances. Her leaping feet splay with the weight of worlds
And beneath that graceful arc
Suns are crushed
Ant hills are flooded
And – I forget...

Forgetting that fluid ballet,
    that still, elegant timeless place,
I imagine there is anywhere I might be
Other than in the power of that vital Dance.

I forget I am composed of patterns
    within a whim of Chaos.

O lucky whim! O Glorious Earth! O Life! O foolishness!
Oh fathomless me who weep and find
This fleshly space a burden.

She lightly floats and all Changes
There is no landing site, there is no loss, there is only Change.
But, I ask, is there this radiant light?
Is Beauty what this bliss,
This laughter, this Brightness is about?
Is "Beauty" Love?

She dances.
I am danced within Her arcing wrist, drawn after the flutter
Of Her trailing Veil.
We are each Her Dark and Light. We are each Love.
We are each flowing powerfully among electrons
Which may be only
Clay being shaped
By the Dance.

About the Author

Born on the Summer Solstice, 1941, Penny June Novack was named after Penelope, Priestess and Queen whose husband, Odysseus, was described in the Greek epic poem "The Odyssey". With her coppery hair and diminutive size at birth, she was immediately dubbed "Penny" and so has been ever since.

Penny entered into service to the Goddess and Witchcraft in 1969 and she and her life-mate, Michael, began organizing Pagan festival events in 1972. In the years since her twelfth birthday when she first entered into her spiritual search, she has studied and enjoyed numerous spiritual paths, and this is still the case. The Goddess is not her jailer but the vast Mystery to be found in every sacred event.

Now a priestess of the Goddess and self-described Fool, she is at the mercy of the Muse, but finds that Source to be healing and revealing rather than a trial. The most difficult thing about being helpless before the pre-emptions of the Muse is the problem of finding something to write on (and with) as the attacks of poetry present themselves.

Penny believes each of you is a poem and that you are filled with light the way a jelly roll is filled with jelly. A toast to the sweetness within you!

On a more mundane level, she resides in the northeastern side of the Massachusetts Berkshires with her mate of 37 years and does gardening and meddling in the lives of her children, grandchildren and friends – among other projects!

www.ingramcontent.com/pod-product-compliance
Lightning Source LLC
Chambersburg PA
CBHW051711040426
42446CB00008B/829